Forgiven the Way of Peace

by
Richard Rice-Oxley
Vicar of St. Matthew's and St. Luke's, Darlington, Co. Durham

GROVE BOOKS LIMITED
Bramcote   Nottingham   NG9 3DS

CONTENTS

PREFACE

This booklet started life as Part 1 of an M.A. thesis at Durham University in 1985. It was revised for a St. John's Durham Extension Course in 1988, and revised again for publication! I am grateful first of all to my tutor at Durham, Ann Loades, to those who took such an active interest in the Extension Course, and most recently to the Grove Books Ethics Group for their helpful advice.

Among many people whom I have talked to about forgiveness I must mention Cecil Kerr of the Renewal Centre at Rostrevor, Northern Ireland. Cecil not only shared his experience, but also enabled me to meet a number of people who had discovered the meaning of forgiveness the hard way.

Finally, my wife Sylvia has supported and encouraged me throughout my studies, and has also done a great deal of typing. Grateful thanks to her and other friends and relatives. God bless you all.

Richard Rice-Oxley
August 1989

THE COVER PICTURE
is by Greg Forster

First Impression October 1989

ISSN 0259-2667
ISBN 1 85174 124 0

INTRODUCTION: THE IMPORTANCE OF FORGIVENESS

Forgiveness stands at the heart of Christian faith and life. Jesus taught his disciples both to ask for and to offer forgiveness. Christians, Sunday by Sunday, state their belief in the forgiveness of sins.

The importance of forgiveness has been stressed by Christian writers through the centuries and thoughtful Christians of the twentieth century have affirmed their verdict. The late Bishop Stephen Neill asserts that 'Forgiveness is at the heart of the universe.'[1] Jean Vanier believes that 'Forgiveness is the greatest factor of growth for any human being.'[2] Peter Hinchliff adds that 'Forgiveness, which is central to Christian faith, is also central to Christian morality.'[3]

But forgiveness is not widely accepted as a valid part of human life. A BBC *Choices* programme in June 1987 was on the subject of the forgiveness of criminals. It was chaired by Rabbi Julia Neuberger. None of her panel of four, nor any of a participating audience, was prepared to state unequivocally the obligation to forgive the sinner. Deputy Chief Constable John Stalker was candid enough to admit that he did not advocate the forgiveness of offenders by their victims in the case of heinous crime. It was more than could be expected of them. A victim of the Moors murders stated she could not forgive, and a psychiatrist lent support with the assertion that hate could be a good emotion if it motivated the victim to action.

Anyone approaching the subject of human forgiveness is confronted with two major questions. First, is forgiveness morally right? That is, are there some deeds so horrendous, such as the holocaust, the Moors murders, etc., that forgiveness is morally reprehensible because it suggests that these acts are less abominable than we actually know them to be? In other words, it is felt that to forgive the offender would be in some way to betray the victim and to connive at the crime.

The second question is a practical one. Even if we allow the moral propriety of forgiving the perpetrators of appalling crime, is it a practical possibility? Are there some people who have been so damaged that, with the best will in the world, they simply cannot find it in them to forgive. Is forgiveness a psychological impossibility for some victims?

Here then are two major challenges to the Christian teaching about forgiveness. One of the main aims of this study will be to give an answer to these challenges. Our approach will not however be that of direct confrontation. It is important to do some groundwork first. Forgiveness, as a moral concept and human activity, is widely misunderstood, even by Christians. Before we try to understand what it is, and when it is appropriate, and how it can be expressed, we must consider certain related but different activities from which it should be clearly distinguished.[4]

---

[1] S. Neill, *A genuinely human existence* (Constable) p.211.
[2] J. Vanier, Address in Canterbury Cathedral September 1983. Quoted by E. de Waal *Seeking God* (Collins, Fount Paperbacks in association with Fount Press, 1984) p.133.
[3] P. Hinchliff, *Holiness and Politics* (Darton, Longman and Todd, 1982) p.59.
[4] This booklet looks at forgiveness between individuals. It lies beyond the scope of our study to consider forgiveness between groups or countries, that is, in the political sphere. For this the reader is referred to *The Forgiveness and Politics Study Project* at 3/35 Buckingham Gate, London SW1E 6PA. There is also some helpful discussion in Lord Longford *Forgiveness of Man by Man* (The Buchebroc Press, 1989).

1. FORGIVENESS AND PARDON

On 27 December 1983, Pope John Paul II (Karol Wojtyla) met the man who had attempted to murder him, Mehmet Ali Agca. The Pope described the meeting in these words:

> 'This will remain as an historic day in my life as a man and a Christian. I was able to meet the person whose name you all know: Ali Agca, who made an attempt on my life.

> 'But providence took things into its own hands in a way I would call exceptional, even marvellous. Today, after more than two years, I was able to meet my assailant and repeat the pardon which I granted immediately to him and which I later expressed from my hospital bed as soon as it was possible.

> 'The Lord allowed us to meet as men and as brothers because all the events of our lives must confirm that God is our Father and all of us are his children in Jesus Christ. Thus we are all brothers.'[1]

This story illustrates a crucial distinction—the difference between pardon and forgiveness. Paragraph 2 shows the Pope, as supreme pontiff, issuing a pardon to an offender. It is the sort of thing you would expect from one who is the official head of the Roman Catholic Church. But in the final paragraph, we have a different picture. The Pope comes down from his position of superiority and meets his attacker as a brother. Although the word 'forgiveness' is not used, forgiveness there must have been, since there is no way he could have referred to Ali Agca as his brother and retained either a cold superiority or an inner attitude of resentment. The Pope, as Pope. pardoned. Karol Wojtyla, as a man, forgave.

The truth is that forgiveness and pardon belong to different logical orders. This point is often obscured by the unfortunate fact that the word 'pardon' can often be used to mean 'forgive'. For instance, in *The Merchant of Venice,* Bassanio, tricked into surrendering the ring given him by Portia, pleads with her:
> 'Portia,. forgive me this enforced wrong.' (5.1.240)

A little later, he tries again:
> 'Pardon this fault, and by my soul I swear
> I never more will break an oath with thee.' (5.1.247-8)[2]

This tendency to use the word 'pardon' in the sense of 'personally forgive' has remained standard English. However, it is quite obvious that the word 'pardon' is used in legal and social contexts which are distinct from the essentially personal world of forgiveness. Because the two words can on occasion be used synonymously, we sometimes fail to make this important conceptual distinction between personal forgiveness and social pardon.

[1] Pope John Paul II: quoted in *The Daily Telegraph*, 28 December 1983.
[2] W. Shakespeare The Merchant of Venice (Oxford Standard Authors edition, ed. W. Craig, O.U.P, 1905).

R. S. Downie in his book *Roles and Values* draws out this distinction most helpfully. First of all, Downie notes, forgiveness is personal. It relates to an injury inflicted on a person, whereas pardoning relates to an offence, the breaking of rules.

Secondly, forgiveness does not deny that a moral wrong has been committed; it is not condonation. Pardon, however, involves letting a person off the 'merited consequences of his actions'. Thirdly, forgiveness is open to anyone who has been injured; pardon is open only to one qualified to condone a breach of the rules, such as a monarch or club chairman. From this it follows that 'I pardon you' is a performative utterance, the word constitutes the deed. But 'I forgive you' may or may not be true—it all depends on the personal attitude of the one speaking.[1]

Of course, the fact that pardoning and forgiving belong to a different logical order does not mean that they cannot be combined in one person. What we need to distinguish is the different activities involved in the one action. We have seen how 'pardon' and 'forgiveness' were beautifully combined in the Pope's approach to his attacker.[2] It also follows that there is nothing illogical in someone personally forgiving and yet wanting an offender to be punished.[3]

Take the case of a man I met in Northern Ireland. Harry McCann from Co. Antrim, had both his legs blown off in a car bomb. He had no hesitation in saying that he completely forgave his assailants in his heart. But he added that if they were ever caught they ought to suffer the full rigour of the law for the crime they had committed.

More recently in 1986, Michael Saward, the Vicar of Ealing, immediately forgave those who broke into his house and savagely beat him up. But he later expressed anger at the leniency of sentences passed on those of his assailants who also raped a young woman in his home. Such anger is entirely justified so long as it is anger against the judicial system, and in no sense directed against the assailants themselves.

Pardon is social, forgiveness is personal. To keep these logically distinct will save us from muddles, and the very real possibility of falsely accusing victims of being unforgiving when all they are doing is maintaining that wrong should be punished, and not condoned.

---

[1] R. S. Downie, *Roles and Values* (Methuen, 1971) pp.151-153.

[2] Of course the Pope does not have the power to remit Ali Acga's punishment. To that extent, the Pope's pardon lacks 'bite'. But we can still envisage a cold 'official' pardon which lacked the warmth of personal forgiveness. The distinction remains valid despite the limited scope of the pardon.

[3] By the same token, it would be quite possible for someone in authority, a judge or monarch, to issue a pardon for an offender, while retaining resentment in his heart against him.

2. FORGIVENESS, UNDERSTANDING AND TOLERANCE

Forgiveness then, unlike pardon, is totally and inescapably personal. From now on, we shall be dealing with the realm of personal relationships. But before we seek to examine the naure of forgiveness itself it is important to distinguish it from other personal activities, which resemble it, but are in some important way different.

Understanding

'Tout comprendre, c'est tout pardonner.'

This French aphorism suggests that total understanding leads inevitably to total forgiveness. If we could fully understand the moods, pressures and motives that have resulted in someone hurting us, we would be bound to forgive him. This viewpoint is taken by Brand Blanshard, a determinist philosopher. While wanting to maintain a judgment against the hurtful act, he says that we must forgive the man who does the act 'with the compassion of one who knows that with the inner and outer forces working upon him at the moment of decision, he could have done no other.'[1]

The same sort of position is taken by psychiatrist R. C. A. Hunter. In one of his case studies he describes a young woman who understands the former attitudes and actions of her parents in a new light after talks with her analyst. She also comes to understand her own faults in a new way. As a result, she stops blaming her parents for their supposed wrongs to her, and thus 'forgives' them. Hunter states: 'What forgiving undoes is the notion or belief that an unjust injury or mischief has been done to oneself, or was intended, which has caused suffering or harm.'[2]

The key to the position described by Blanshard, the philosopher, and Hunter, the psychiatrist, is that understanding leads to the removal of blame from the offending person. It is interesting that earlier in his article Hunter actually calls forgiveness 'the opposite of blaming.'[3]

But to identify understanding and forgiveness in this way is unacceptable. Very often a full understanding of the situation leads to the inescapable conclusion that the wrongdoer was fully responsible for his actions and very much to blame. What Blanshard and Hunter have been describing is excusing, the removal of blame, which thus makes forgiveness unnecessary. C. S. Lewis expresses the point forcefully.

'There is all the difference in the world between forgiving and excusing. Forgiveness says: "Yes, you have done this thing, but I accept your apology, I will never hold it against you and everything between us two will be exactly as it was before." But excusing says: "I see that you couldn't help it, or didn't mean it, you weren't really to blame." If one was not really to blame then there is nothing to forgive. In that sense forgiveness and excusing are almost opposites.'[4]

[1] B. Blanchard, 'Reply to Elizabeth L. Beardsley' in P. Schlipp (ed.), *The Philosophy of Brand Blanshard* (Library of Living Philosophers, Open Court, 1980) p.263.
[2] R. C. A. Hunter, 'Forgiveness, retaliation and paranoid reactions' in *Canadian Psychiatry Association Journal* Vol. 23 (1978) pp.168-169. The quotation is from p.169.
[3] R. C. A. Hunter, p.167.
[4] C. S. Lewis, 'On forgiveness', in *Fern-seeds and elephants* (ed. W. Hooper) (Collins, Fount paperbacks, 1975) p.40.

It seems that Lewis is right to make this distinction between forgiving and excusing, as against Hunter and Blanshard. But in life the distinction sometimes becomes rather blurred. One such case is that of Mary Sandys, whose 17-year-old son was knocked off his bike, and killed, by a lorry. It was a complete accident—if anything the lad was to blame. Yet the lorry driver still felt the need to ask Mary to forgive him, and she still felt it appropriate to say 'I forgive you', not 'I excuse you—it was an accident.' Both the driver and the mother accepted that, as he was in charge of the vehicle, he was in some sense responsible for the death. And Mary's forgiveness did not mean 'ceasing to blame' but rather 'letting go of resentment'. We shall look at the whole question of resentment later on.

So understanding, excusing and forgiving are not to be identified as the same thing. However, we must allow that understanding often plays an important part in enabling a person to forgive. As Charles Williams says, 'To forgive another involves, sooner or later, so full an understanding of the injury, and its cause, that in some sense we have committed the injury; we are that which injures ourselves.'[1] This sounds very similar to what Blanshard is saying, but there is an important difference. Blanshard posits a situation where the injured party understands that his injurer could do no other than hurt him. Williams seems to be talking about an understanding which sympathetically enters into the weakness which led to the injury, but which does not thereby seek to exonerate the injurer.

An example of understanding which leads to forgiveness comes in the short story 'A Bar of Shadow', by Laurens van de Post.[2] This concerns the relationship between Hara, a Japanese officer in a prisoner-of-war camp and Lawrence, a British officer, who suffered terrible beatings at his hands. There is never any question that Hara was guilty of these and many other offences, including murder. But Lawrence understands that they were committed from a genuine desire to do what was right according to the morality to which Hara adhered. Basically Hara thought that to be taken alive was a shocking 'crime', and that his brutality was therefore fully justified, even required, to correct the 'wrong-thinking' of his enemies. Because of his deep understanding of this Japanese morality, Lawrence does not blame Hara for his actions. Even while he was suffering he felt sorry for him, and after the war, at the war trial, he pleaded for Hara's life:

> 'It seemed to me just as wrong for us now to condemn Hara under a law which had never been his, or which he had never even heard, as he and his masters had been to punish and kill us for transgressions of the code of Japan that was not ours'.[3]

We note that Lawrence does not excuse Hara completely. He says he was wrong to try and impose his morality on the British. But Lawrence's understanding of an alien morality is such that he refuses to feel malice against the man who hurt him or accept that the death penalty is suitable

---

[1] C. Williams, *He came down from heaven* and *The forgiveness of sins* (Faber & Faber, 1950) p.189.
[2] L. van der Post, 'A Bar of Shadow' in *The Seed and the Sower* (The Hogarth Press, 1963; Penguin edition, 1966) pp.7-38.
[3] L. van der Post, *The Seed and the Sower*, p.34.

for one who was only doing right by his own lights. Hara and Lawrence meet face to face and are reconciled in Hara's prison cell on the night before he is hanged. There is an ironic twist at the end of the story. Lawrence feels the need for *personal* forgiveness in European terms, whereas it is clear that Hara is quite content with the rather formal encounter between the two men. Lawrence's deep understanding of their different views of wrong does not seem to be matched by a corresponding insight into their different understandings of forgiveness.[1]

Tolerance

Tolerance refuses to judge or condemn the hurt from the outset, accepting it as if it were not wrong. Such a reaction to minor faults is often the most practical solution. 'A soft answer turns away wrath' is an example of how a tolerant response to provocation may defuse a potentially damaging dispute. Tolerance, however, has its limitations, as John Wisdom shows.[2]

For one thing, such tolerance may be false. A man may deceive others, and even himself, into thinking that he has not taken offence, but in fact underneath he may be nursing resentment. This sort of tolerance seems akin to the sort of forgiveness described by Hunter as a 'reaction formation', a defence against vengeful aggression. Here the tolerance/forgiveness is the psyche's way of dealing with vengeful feelings which the hurt person is not willing to express.

Tolerance may be foolish. No good can come in the long term from pretending that a hurtful act was not really so wrong after all. If not quite as bad as calling 'evil good', it blurs an essential moral distinction upon which the health of society depends.

Tolerance of a hurt to oneself may involve others, and result in hurting them. Thus a host's tolerance of a boorish member of his dinner-party may ruin the evening for the remainder of his guests. Perhaps the older brother in the parable of the Prodigal Son mistook his Father's forgiveness for tolerance, an easy acceptance of the younger son's misdemeanours. If so, he was right to protest. (There were, of course, other less creditable reasons for his outburst).

The most damaging indictment of tolerance is that it often indicates a refusal to respond to what has happened in a fully personal way. As Wisdom points out, a tolerant attitude to the hurts inflicted on him may indicate that a man has too little regard for himself. Thus in ancient Greece a slave might tolerate appalling hurt and injury simply because he did not value himself hihgly enough to resent them. Or today, racial minorities may tolerate racial prejudice because deep down they do not feel they deserve anything else.

Tolerance of wrong may also indicate that a person has too little regard for the one who has hurt them. 'Even a remorseful sinner who has screwed up the courage to apologize is not looking for tolerance', writes Helen Oppenheimer. 'The calm acknowledgement that one just is that sort of person may be less alarming than bitter reproaches, but is not really sustaining.'[2]

[1] See L. van der Post, *The Seed and the Sower*, pp.36-38.
[2] J. Wisdom, 'Tolerance', in *Paradox and Discovery* (Blackwell, 1965), pp.139-147.
[3] H. Oppenheimer, *The Hope of Happiness* (SCM, 1983), p.119.

There is a good example of this in Iris Murdoch's novel, *The Red and the Green* which is set in Ireland in 1916.

Barney has decided to confess two 'wrongs' which he has been committing against his wife, Kathleen—visiting another woman, and writing a derogatory diary of their relationship. He finds that his wife knows about the former and couldn't care less about the latter. The writer goes on:
> 'Barney had often imagined himself making this confession to Kathleen, but it had been in a scene quite unlike this one. He had pictured himself shaken by emotion the words rent from his breast. He had pictured Kathleen's stricken face, perhaps her tears, her bitter reproaches, and then the great reconciliation. But this was as random and senseless as the sea roaring through the rocks.'[1]

There is more than one reason for the failure of Barney's confession. He has chosen the wrong time, with his wife preoccupied with her son's likely involvement in the Easter rising, and the wrong place, a crowded bus shelter lacking the necessary privacy.

However, the main reason for Barney's failure is his wife's tolerance of his faults. Barney saw his visits to Millie as an act of unfaithfulness, Kathleen did not. Barney saw his derogatory remarks about her in his diary as wrong, Kathleen did not.

Kathleen's reaction shows the poor quality of her relationship with her husband. Had she expected more of it, she might have been hurt. Had she been hurt, the confession might have seemed appropriate and forgiveness possible. Because she did not really care what her husband did, no offence was taken and Barney was left deeply confused. In fact a refusal to forgive might have been better for him than such a clear demonstration of his wife's failure to be related to him as a wife to a husband. So mere tolerance can be even worse than unforgiveness.

Forgiveness, then, goes beyond both understanding and tolerance. It looks hurt squarely in the face, and acknowledges it to be wrong, and the agent responsible. As Lewis says,
> 'Real forgiveness means looking steadily at the sin, the sin that is left over without any excuse, after all allowances have been made, and seeing it in all its horror, dirt, meanness and malice, and nevertheless being wholly reconciled to the man who has done it.'[1]

But is reconciliation in these circumstances morally justifiable?

[1] I. Murdoch, *The Red and the Green* (1965; Triad/Panther, 1978) p.198.
[2] C. S. Lewis p.42.

3. THE MORAL JUSTIFICATION OF FORGIVENESS

'Forgiveness', said Bernard Shaw, 'is a beggar's refuge; we must all pay our debts.'[1] Shaw was expressing in his usual pungent way what many believe—that forgiveness as defined at the end of our last section is basically immoral. If a man has wilfully and knowingly committed a wrong against another, surely the unconditional forgiveness of the wrong is really condonation of it—the wolf of tolerance dressed in the sheep's clothing of forgiveness?

Perhaps the most stringent expression of this view is by the philosopher Elizabeth Beardsley. She argues that the only good reason for forgiving a wrongdoer his act is 'favourable moral appraisal', that is, the understanding that the agent acted from a morally good desire, or motive, however the act itself appeared. Later she adds that she believes that there is no 'duty of forgiveness', not even a *prima facie* duty. Forgiveness is a response which is, or is not, deserved, an attitude the adoption of which in a given case has (or lacks) a good reason. The only justification is whether X had a morally good motive in performing A.[2]

This is an extreme position, not widely held among philosophers, but it arises from a genuine desire not to compromise with evil. Is forgiveness morally defensible? For answer let us turn first to another philosopher, Hannah Arendt. She points out that the consequence of following the Beardsley viewpoint is the death of human relationships:

> 'Trespassing' is an everyday occurrence inevitable in the course of human action and needs forgiving and dismissing so that life can go on. Revenge is the natural response to trespass. But it is a reacting to the original action which keeps everyone bound to the consequences of the first misdeed and the consequent chain reaction. By contrast, the act of forgiving cannot be predicted and thus retains something of the freedom of the original action. It 'acts anew and unexpectedly, unconditioned by the act which provoked it and therefore freeing from its consequences both the one who forgives and the one who is forgiven.[3]

Theologian H. R. Mackintosh also remarks on the creative and renewing nature of forgiveness, which proves that it is morally justifiable. 'It (forgiveness) cannot be immoral, for it calls out a new and victorious goodness. The difficulty of understanding it lies in the fact that it is creative.'[4]

[1] Quoted by H. R. Mackintosh,*The Christian Experience of Forgiveness,* (Nisbet and Co., 1927; Fontana Books, 1961) p.184.
[2] E. L. Beardsley, 'Understanding and forgiveness' in P. Schlipp, ed., *The Philosophy of Brand Blanshard* pp.251-254.
[3] H. Arendt, *The Human Condition* University of Chicago Press, 1958), pp.240-241. The quotation is from p.241. The writer is not suggesting that Beardsley is advocating revenge. But the failure to forgive any sort of intentional wrongs, which she advocates, would have similar 'binding' effects on human relationships. Arendt herself seems not to appreciate the full scope of forgiveness, limiting it to ignorant guilt, and excluding 'crime and willed evil', the forgiving of which is particularly liberating and creative.
[4] H. R. Mackintosh, p.184.

Stephen Neill agrees, asserting that 'Forgiveness is always creative; it brings into being a totally new situation; it is hardly an exaggeration to say that it brings into being a new world.'[1]

The second moral justification of forgiveness was first hinted at by Joseph Butler in his sermon 'Upon forgiveness of injuries'. He points out that anger or hatred tend to make us condemn the whole of a man's character rather than just the aspect which has offended us.[2] Neill draws out the implication of these words when he observes that 'the offender has done wrong, about this there can be no pretence. But that is not the whole truth about him. He is still of infinite value as a person ...'[3] This is a very important point. It is a person who has to be forgiven, a person who is very much more than the offence he has committed, however terrible it may have been. To refuse to forgive is tantamount to rejecting the person entirely. In a telling phrase, Arendt speaks of forgiving the 'what' for the 'who'. 'Forgiving', she writes, 'is always an eminently personal affair in which what was done is forgiven for the sake of who did it.'[4] Love is concerned with who the loved person is, rather than what the person has or has not done. Thus it is sometimes thought that only love has the power to forgive. But in the wider sphere of human affairs, respect should ensure forgiveness, because it is offered to people irrespective of qualities or achievements we may approve of.[5]

The Place of Repentance

But surely one vital factor in the moral justification of forgiveness has been omitted—repentance on the part of the wrongdoer? If he acknowledges that what he has done is wrong and seeks to make amends, then forgiveness is justified. But if he does not repent, if he continues on his way oblivious to his wrong, or even worse, callously indifferent to it, then surely to forgive must be to condone?

Moberly expresses this view forcefully: 'Forgiveness, then, . . . if it is to be that real forgiveness which is the spontaneous action of righteousness, and not that indifference to sin which is itself a new sin; is strictly and absolutely correlative to what may be called the "forgiveableness" of the person forgiven.' Later he adds, 'Either he is forgiveable, or he is not. So far as he is not I ought to forgive. . . . One for whom I am responsible, defies all right and exalts in his defiance. And I, refusing to punish, receive him with open arms as righteous and good. Then, in still more directness of sense, the sin, without ceasing to be on his side, has come over to mine. I have but identified myself wiuth his wickedness.'[6] 'We may', says J. R. Lucas, 'urge a man who has been wronged by another not to keep thinking about it, because although it was a grievous wrong, there are many other better

[1] S. Neill, p.213.
[2] J. Butler, 'Upon Forgiveness of Injuries' in Butler's *Fifteen Sermons* (ed. T. A. Roberts) (SPCK, 1970) para. 23; pp.80-89.
[3] S. Neill, p.210.
[4] H. Arendt, p.241. A similar point is made by H. A. Williams, 'Theology and self-awareness' in A. R. Vidler (ed.) *Soundings* (Cambridge, 1962) p.98.
[5] H. Arendt, pp.242-243.
[6] R. C. Moberly, *Atonement and Personality* (John Murray, 1909).

things to think about, and he ought not to dwell unnecessarily on unprofitable topics. But we cannot urge him to forgive him so long as he has not disowned his action and sought forgiveness.'[1]

These statements seem such obvious good sense, that it might appear foolhardy to question them, but question them we must, and on two counts. First of all, the position of Moberly and Lucas seems to rule out the possibility of forgiving the (unrepentant) dead. Yet it is the experience of many people that they do genuinely come to forgive people who have hurt them, after they have died. Such forgiveness is obviously not in any way related to their repentance. The same thing applies to those who forgive unknown assailants. In the mid-seventies Joseph Parker, a Belfast minister, lost his 14-year-old son in a bomb blast. The only way he could identify his son's body was by his watch. Yet the next day Joseph Parker published the following message to his son's murderers in a Belfast newspaper: 'Whoever you are, I forgive you.'

More recently we have the example of Gordon Wilson. Interviewed on television after the murder of his daughter in the Enniskillen bombing of 8 November 1987, he declared: 'My wife Joan and I do not bear any grudges. We do not hold any ill-will against those responsible for this. I shall pray for those people tonight and every night. God forgive them, for they know not what they do.' Such a response to heinous crime is by no means uncommon in Ireland. Are we to call it immoral?

Secondly the insistence that forgiveness must always be preceded by repentance rules out the possibility of forgiveness inducing repentance. Yet sometimes this is what happens. For example Fr. Dimitri Dudko, a Russian Orthodox priest, tells the story of the change that came over an atheist in prison. He had attempted to break the faith of a Baptist Christian who shared the same cell, and had succeeded in reducing the Christian to tears, as he prayed for God's strength in his time of trial. Then, in the prisoner's own words;

> 'Suddenly he looked at me and smiled. I was amazed at his face: there was something joyous about it, pure, as though it had just been washed clean. *The weight immediately fell from my soul. I understood that he had forgiven me.*' (my italics)

> 'And then a light of some sort penetrated me, and I understood that God existed. It was not even so much that I understood, but rather i sensed it with my whole being. He is everywhere. He is our Father! We are his children, brothers one to another. I forgot that I was in prison and felt only one thing—a great joy and thankfulness to the Lord who had revealed himself to me, who was unworthy.'[2]

Of course, we recognize that there is a balance to be struck. Forgiveness which actually precludes repentance is foolish, if not immoral. The repentance of the wrongdoer, if that is possible, must always be sought by the forgiver, for without it the true end of forgiveness, personal reconciliation, is impossible.

[1] J. R. Lucas, 'Forgiveness' in *Freedom and Grace* (SPCK, 1976) p.83.
[2] M. Bourdeaux, *Risen Indeed* (Darton, Longman and Todd/St. Vladimir's Seminary Press, 1983), pp89-90.

Aurel Kolnai wrestles with this problem. and makes some good points. He sees forgiveness as a 'generous venture of trust', morally wrong only if there is no prospect whatever of the wrongdoer repenting. He argues that the situation which makes forgiveness legitimate and virtuous is that in which the forgiver has some reason to hope for a change of heart by the wrongdoer. The fact that his hope may be disappointed does not invalidate his forgiveness. It expresses the attitude of trust which may increase the trustworthiness of the recipient. This involves a 'risk'. His 'gamble' may be wise, dubious, or frankly unwise (where malice takes advantage of the good-natured approach). On some occasions we may disapprove of the forgiver's attitude without denying that it is genuine forgiveness, or condemning it as condonation.[1]

As Kolnai indicates, such a 'generous venture of trust' can be exploited by the morally unscrupulous. An example is given by psychiatist Paul Tournier in his first book *The Healing of Persons*. A woman whom he calls Cecile had tried to commit suicide following years of matrimonial problems. After several long conversations, Cecile accepted God and also her unsatisfactory marriage. 'But,' says Tournier,
> 'the matrimonial situation was no better. The contrary, in fact, was the case. The husband seemed to find it very convenient to have a wife who was ready to put with everything and accept everything without ceasing to love him. His attitude toward her reminded me of a cat playing with a mouse. He would leave her and then come back to her without a word of regret, take advantage of what she had earned, and then leave her again. Despite her communion with God, the poor woman had more sorrow than joy.'[2]

This particular story had a happy ending. The husband eventually came to his senses and the marriage was reborn. But what of those whose forgiving love meets no answering response? Should they continue to forgive? Would not resentment be a more natural, even more moral, attitude in the circumstances?

[1] A. Kolnai, 'Forgiveness' in *Proceedings of the Aristotelian Society* 79 (New Series 1973-4), pp.89-90.
[2] P. Tournier, The Healing of Persons (trans. E. Hudson), (Collins, 1966), pp.90-92.

4. RESENTMENT

Bishop Joseph Butler's discussion of resentment in Sermons 8 and 9 provide a useful starting point for our consideration of the subject.

In Sermon 8, 'Upon Resentment', he makes the point that resentment (by which he evidently means moral indignation) against a wrong act is justified as an appropriate response to what has happened. It is the abuses of resentment that are morally wrong, e.g. malice and revenge (§2) or resentment against an imagined injury (§10). And it is not only 'sudden' anger, the instinctive response to injury which is justifiable. 'Deliberate' resentment is also justified when its purpose is to prevent and remedy injury (§7).

In Sermon 9, 'Upon Forgiveness of Injuries', Butler maintains that the precepts to 'forgive' and to 'love our enemies' cannot forbid the justifiable indignation we feel at injury, but only the excess and abuse of this natural feeling(§3). Resentment, he goes on, is not inconsistent with goodwill: we may love our enemy and yet have resentment against him for the injuries he has done us (§13). A man should love his enemies not with any kind of affection, but feeling towards them as 'a just and impartial spectator would feel'. So forgiving enemies is neither impracticable nor unreasonable.

Stephen Sykes, in a sermon accepts Butler's position:

> 'If we agree with Butler, and I do, we do not say first to those with ample cause to hate their enemies, that they ought to forgive, bless and love them; but rather that there is a proper role for resentment, as indignation against injury and wickedness—that to experience such indignation is not . . . regrettable and that it is natural and right to experience it in proportion to the degree of evil, designed or premeditated.'

He continues:

> 'What then is forgiveness? . . . It cannot, if resentment is proper and justified, be the elaborate pretence that one is not resentful. It must, therefore, refer to a willingness to allow resentment only within the bounds of a conception of a common good; a steady desire that some good . . . whole community be brought out of evil, even out of great wickedness.'[1]

Butler and Sykes then see resentment and forgiveness as in some way compatible. Other philosophers regard them as mutually exclusive. For example Downie agrees that resentment is a natural response to injury but adds that it ought to be 'replaced by forgiveness'.[2] Beardsley describes forgiveness as 'the withdrawal of reentment'.[3] Stephen Neill castigates resentment as one of the three great 'enemies' of mankind.

> '(Resentment) is the most toxic of all the ills that can assail the human spirit. In many cases it is possible to see the venom that it distils and to trace its harmful effects on every part of the inner constitution of man. . . . Clean wounds heal quickly, the festering wound never heals. The festering wound is the symbol of that injury that ha s been met with resentful indignation.'[4]

[1] S. Sykes, 'Forgiveness and Resentment' (Sermon in Durham Cathedral, 1981) p.2 and p.3.
[2] R. S. Downie, p.150.
[3] E. Beardsley, p.252.
[4] S. Neill, pp.207-208.

Here we appear to have a serious clash of views, but it is more apparent than real. The word 'resentment' itself is partly to blame. As used by Butler and Sykes it refers primarily to the moral indignation felt as the initial reaction to an injury. But Neill is using the word to refer to a settled attitude of antipathy towards someone, resulting from some injury. continuing for a long period, damaging one's own psychological and spiritual well-being.

A metaphor used by Helen Oppenheimer may help here 'Snow', she says, 'is a good analogy for grievance ... Newly fallen snow is insubstantial stuff, melting as it lands when the ground is warm ... But when it has settled and been trodden down it is solid and dangerous and can break bones.'[1] So we can accept the validity of initial resentment, but we must beware of that resentful attitude lingering for too long. It can be highly damaging.

Esther de Waal agrees: 'It is only too easy to keep up an internal conversation by which I chew over that hurting remark, or that undeserved happening, or I refuse to forget some slight, or I go on saying "It isn't fair" ... to myself. Then what began as quite a small grudge or resentment has been nursed into a great brooding cloud that smothers all my inner landscape, or has become a cancer eating up more and more of my inner self.'[2]

This reference to cancer is interesting. since it was echoed by a number of the people I met in Ireland in October 1984. David Hamilton for instance, a former member of the Ulster Volunteer Force (UVF), spoke of his hatred as 'a cancerous growth' in him. A woman we shall call Bridget had had a long-standing feud with her brother. Two years of legal battles to gain her rightful share of the family home took their toll and she was left with a deep-seated hatred of her brother, which she said was, 'eating away at me like a cancer'. So obsessive was her hatred that she felt she had lost her personality. 'I felt I didn't exist as a person'.

Cecil Kerr is the Director of the Christian Renewal Centre in Rostrevor, Co. Down, border town in Northern Ireland. He meets many people who are grappling with the problem of resentment. One was a policeman who had been ambushed by the IRA and injured. Several of his friends had been killed. He knew who the men were, and he was determined to get them. But his resentment was affecting him physically; it was, said Cecil, 'eating him up'. Another woman he knew was bitterly resentful towards her in-laws. He warned her that if she continued to hold that resentment she might suffer from arthritis. This woman actually visited the centre during our stay and Cecil Kerr confirmed that arthritis was beginning to set in. The drying up of the bones was the body's response to the drying up of the spirit caused by deep-seated resentment.

So are resentment and forgiveness in any way compatible? I think not. Both are valid responses to injury. But forgiveness means the withdrawal of resentment. It is not enough for resentment to be contained—it must be removed completely. Forgiveness must follow resentment. If it does not, the injured person is simply adding a self-inflicted wound to the one they have already received from another.

[1] H. Oppenheimer, 'Grievances' (University Sermon, preached on Sunday, 1 May 1983, at Great St. Mary's Church, Cambridge), p.5.
[2] E. de Waal, p.133.

5. OTHER REASONS FOR FORGIVING

The second reason to forgive is that in many cases the wrongdoer desperately needs to be forgiven. Even very small misdemeanours can weigh on a person's conscience, and the words 'Never mind, I forgive you' can bring great relief. Of course sometimes people are guilty of terrible crimes against others, and repentance leads to a sense of shame and a longing to confess and be forgiven.

Lewis Smedes in *Forgive and Forget* tells the story of Michael Christopher's play 'The Black Angel'. It is about a German General Herman Eingel who is sentenced to 30 years imprisonment for war crimes in World War II. Following his release his hideout is tracked down by a Frenchman, Morrieaux, whose whole family had been massacred by Eingel's army. Morrieaux had planned Eingel's death, but after meeting him relents and offers to help him escape. Yet this is not enough for Eingel—he wants to be forgiven. This Morrieaux will not, or perhaps cannot, do. Smedes quotes the story to show how pervasive is long-nursed bitterness. But it shows something else—how vital is the need to be forgiven. It was more important to Eingel than saving his life.[1]

Thirdly, as Smedes points out, to refuse to forgive a person on the grounds that he is too evil is to suggest that his wrongdoing effectively places him outside the scope of normal human relationships. 'In other words, we are turning the wrongdoer into either a sub-human or superhuman monster. Yet unlike the Devil, no human being is purely evil. He or she is always more than his evil act, or acts, however terrible. A human is a being created by God, loved by God, and capable of being forgiven—by God and man.

The last reason why we should forgive the wrongdoer is simply that in the Lord's prayer Jesus tells us to forgive those who sin against us. Indeed he links it with God's forgiveness of us. In Mark 11.25, he says: 'And when you stand praying, if you have a grievance against anyone, forgive him, so that your father in heaven may forgive you the wrongs you have done.'

Corrie ten Boom, a Dutch woman, had been imprisoned by the Germans in Ravensbruck Concentration Camp. Her sister had died in the camp. After the war, Corrie ten Boom went round Germany preaching to Germans that God forgives. In Munich she was approached by one of the most cruel guards in the camp. The guard told Corrie that he had turned to Christ and received God's forgiveness. He wanted *her* forgiveness too, and held out his hand. This was too much for Corrie. She remembered her sister's painful death, and 'froze'. Yet she also remembered the Lord's command to forgive. Knowing that forgiveness was not a feeling, but an act of will, she prayed:

> 'Jesus, help me! . . . I can lift my hand. I can do that much. You supply the feeling. . . . And so woodenly, mechanically, I thrust my hand into the one stretched out to me. And as I did, an incredible thing took place. The current started in my shoulder, raced down my arm, sprang into our joined hands. And then this healing warmth seemed to flood my whole being, bringing tears to my eyes. "I forgive you, brother!" I cried. "With all my heart".'[1]

[1] L. Smedes: *Forgive and forget* (Triangle/SPCK, 1988) pp.24-5.
[2] L. Smedes, pp.80-81.
[3] C. ten Boom, *Tramp for the Lord* (Hodder and Stoughton and Christian Literature Crusade, 1974; 1975 edition) pp.56-57.

6. THE PROCESS OF FORGIVENESS

Smedes lists four stages in forgiving—we hurt, we hate, we heal ourselves, we come together.[1] This process was vividly illustrated in the experience of 'Bridget', whom we have mentioned above. The longstanding quarrel with her brother left her so hurt that she nursed a deep-seated hatred for him. 'I hated him with every bone of my body'. Stage three, healing herself, was a long and difficult process. It started with God challenging her to pray for her brother, and her priest encouraging her that God would help her to forgive. But this was not enough. She also needed the supportive prayers of a Christian community, and a crucial moment. One day she attended a healing service at The Christian Renewal Centre at Rostrevor, Co. Down. The leader, Cecil Kerr, told the worshippers to bring to mind people they could not forgive, to bring them on their hands and release them to God. 'Bridget' brought her brother in her hands, saying, 'Lord, I want to forgive my brother, but I can't. I want to forgive him completely and forget the past.' The result was staggering: 'Before the end of the service I started to cry and cry. I hadn't cried for 15 years. I felt as if the tears were coming up from the tips of my toes. There was a great release, all my burdens were lifted, and I could smile and laugh again.' She wrote to her brother warmly, telling him of her concern for him. She received a warm and loving letter back. What of Stage four? Well, I am not sure how the relationship has developed. Bridget was honest enough to admit that her forgiveness did not mean she could live in the same house as her brother. Forgiveness is an attitude of heart, and the 'coming together' will vary in intimacy according to the personalities of those involved, and of course, the willingness of the other partly to be reconciled.

While Smedes' analysis of the four stages of forgiveness is helpful, it is not true of all cases. Stage two 'we hate' is often missed out. I don't believe that Joseph Parker or Gordon Wilson hated the people who murdered their children. What is more, the hurting and forgiving doubtless went on simultaneously. The fact that they instantly forgave did not mean that they ceased to suffer pain.

Forgiveness of deep wounds may take time. We have already seen that for 'Bridget' there was a slow process of forgiveness. Where injuries are deep, and more important, resentment has been allowed to settle, it may take years. Liam McCluskey, an IRA hunger-striker, had been praying for 18 months for the ability to forgive his enemies. Only after the hunger strike was over, and he had made his peace with God, was he given the 'grace' to forgive.

Sometimes help is needed. Paul Mckeown, whose 20-year-old daughter Karen was shot in a tit-for-tat murder in Belfast, was taught to forgive by her daughter herself before she died. Karen said she felt only pity for the lad who did it. Once her mother was at her bedside, looking very dejected. 'Mam', said Karen, 'you go home and think about *his* Mam.' Later Pearl confirmed that she had no feelings of bitterness towards the lad. 'How do you feel about him?' she was asked. 'More than sorry', was her reply, 'I pray daily that he will repent.'

[1] L. Smedes, p.2.

Sometimes people have too much to cope with to be able to afford the extra burden of resentment. Harry McCann, the man whose legs were blown off in a car bomb, prayed in the ambulance: 'May God forgive the people who have done this. I'm going to die.' From then on he was too pre-occupied with making his peace with God, and recovering from his physi-cal injuries, to give time to resentment. 'There was never any question of my not forgiving' he said. But he admitted that his wife found it a lot harder to forgive than he did.

Most of us do not experience drastic traumas of this nature. We live in a world of little hurts. But such little hurts are not always easy to forgive, especially when they are repeated. 'It is perhaps not so hard to forgive a single great injury,' writes Lewis, 'but to forgive the incessant pro-vocations of daily life—to keep on forgiving the bossy mother-in-law, the bullying husband, the nagging wife, the selfish daughter, the deceitful son—how can we do it?'[1] Such forgiveness will be less spectacular than that of the single great wrong, but it may actually demand more strength of character. Failure at this mundane level has led to many a broken marriage, and many an unhappy home. However difficult the repeated forgiveness of the 'incessant provocations of daily life', it must be acknow-ledged to be absolutely essential to harmonious personal relationships.

[1] C. S. Lewis, p.43.

7. MUTUAL FORGIVENESS

In many situations when forgiveness is the remedy, both parties are at fault. Here there is a need for mutual forgiveness, a recognition that the blame for what has happened cannot be placed wholly on the shoulders of one person.

This is frequently true in marital disputes, which can often be resolved by mutual forgivness. As William Cowper says:
  'The humblest and the happiest pair
  Will find occasion to forbear
  And something, every day they live
  To pity, and perhaps forgive![1]

A delightful example of mutual forgiveness in marriage comes to us from the late Festo Kivengere, an African Bishop:
  'It was after midnight and I was *still* awake. My wife was peacefully sleeping. In my thoughts I was taking her to court and accusing her. I said, "Yes, Lord, she is really wrong this time." "But she is soundly asleep," the Lord said to me, "and you are still in court. Do you mean that it is the holy people that don't sleep? *You* are wrong. Won't you accept it?" In the end I had to say, "Yes, Lord, I was wrong, but what shall I do?" "Early in the morning ask her forgiveness for your attitude." I said, "What if she doesn't accept it?" He asked, "You leave that to me, just do your part." So early in the morning I woke her up. Hesitantly, I said, "I'm sorry about the hardness of last night ..." At first she wondered if I meant business, but then I said, "Please forgive me." She did forgive me, bless her. Immediately the Lord removed the barrier. "I'm sorry too," she said. "I was rather fussy about the thing." And I said, "'No, it wasn't your fault." Laughing she said, "No it wasn't your fault either." And we were in each others' arms, forgiven by each other and the Lord.'[2]

Poet William Blake wrote again and again about mutual forgiveness, as in the following instances.
  'Mutual forgiveness of each vice
  Such are the Gates of Paradise.'

                                        (The Gates of Paradise)

  'And throughout all eternity
  I forgive you, you forgive me.

  This is Jerusalem in every man
  A Tent and Tabernacle of Mutual forgiveness.' *(Jerusalem)*[3]

Sometimes 'Jerusalem' is a lost city because people are prepared to forgive, but see nothing in their behaviour that requires the forgiveness of the other. As Williams wisely comments, 'Many reconciliations have unfortunately broken down because both parties have come prepared to forgive and unprepared to be forgiven.'[4]

---

[1] Quoted by D. and V. Mace, *Love and Anger in Marriage* (Zondervan Corporation, 1982; Pickering and Inglis, 1983) p.71.
[2] F. Kivengere, 'King of our Home' in *African Enterprise Outlook* (December, 1983) p.1.
[3] All quotations from V. Gollancz, *From Darkness to Light* (Abridged edition, V. Gollancz Ltd., 1964), pp.310-311.
[4] C. Williams, p.193.

However, when both parties do acknowledge their faults the effect can be dramatic. This was the case with Ken Hatano, a young Japanese sent by his church to Papua New Guinea. He was part of a team of Christians dedicated to bringing reconciliation between Japanese and Papuans, who had been adversaries in World War II.

Problems came when Ken met an Australian doctor who constantly reminded him of Japanese war crimes. Ken who had not even been born at the time of World War II, felt very resentful but suppressed his feelings. One day they went to see a famous landmark, a church tower and cross which had survived when the church itself was destroyed by Japanese shells. As they posed arm in arm for a photograph, in front of the 'miracle' cross, something happened.

'Up to that point I still felt this suppressed rage. I couldn't say anything kind or loving or humble. But an impulse to speak overwhelmed me, an almost physical stimulus coming from the cross behind me. I had to speak. I blurted out: "The war *was* terrible. And we were to blame. Forgive us!"

'And all at once he was clinging to me, weeping and saying "No, no, it's for you to forgive me!" I could hardly believe it. This tough, seasoned Aussie in tears! All the resentment that had been building up inside me evaporated. Hate, jealousy, rage, melted away. It was a moment of total reconciliation, in front of the miracle cross. I shall never forget that moment.'[1]

Mutual forgiveness is rarely so dramatic as this, but its manifestation in the ordinary affairs of human life is just as important. How often do disputes between individuals, or even communities, drag on because each party insists on looking only at the right on its side, and fails to see the right on the other side. A generosity of spirit, and willingness to own up to whatever part we may have had in a quarrel, however small, can sometimes unblock the logjam. But where hurts run deep, it may need a 'miracle cross' to shift it.

[1] K. Hatano, *Report on the Japan-Papua New Guinea Work Project, February, 1979* (Published under the title 'Reconciled' in *Decision* magazine, October 1980).

8. THE RESULTS OF FORGIVENESS

(a) Forgiveness and Healing

Resentment, however justified, when permitted to persist, is detrimental to a person's mental, spiritual and even physical well-being. Forgiveness, the 'letting-go' of this resentment, often means a profound healing, always psychologically, and sometimes physically as well.

As Neill writes, 'If resentment is the most toxic of the ills the flesh is heir to, forgiveness, the act of forgiving, the willingness to forgive, is the most potent, the most rapid, the most efficacious in its working of all known remedies.'[1] Forgiveness, as a healing power, is borne out by doctors and those involved in spiritual healing. Francis Macnutt, a Roman Catholic priest who is an authority on spiritual healing, writes of an occasion when, at a communal penance service, he spoke of the need fo forgive enemies and then gave his listeners time to respond. This was followed by a prayer for inner healing, but physical healing was not mentioned. Yet, after the service, a man who had just forgiven his boss found that the pain in his chest resulting from open-heart surgery had been completely removed.[1]

Mitchell and Anderson, in their book about the experience of loss, refer to the tendency to hang on to resentment after divorce. 'In order to keep alive the resentment that legitimates the divorce, positive memories may be excluded altogether. The one who holds tight to the posture of victim can only remember what is negative or painful about the marriage in order to preserve the myth of having been victimized. Such selective remembering also precludes the possibility of forgiveness that can bring healing to those memories.'

Mitchell and Anderson then quote the story of Megan, who was seeing a counsellor following her divorce. For more than six months, Megan slated her husband as a psychopath, a liar, a cruel man. The counsellor asked her for a picture of her husband. Eventually a photo album was produced. It showed the love between Megan and her former husband, and her obvious dependence on him. The counsellor remarked: 'It must be difficult to hold in your mind the image of a strong, dependable, psychopathic bully.' Megan began to laugh, and laughed till she cried. Then she saw both sides of her husband—it was the beginning of healing.[3]

Corrie ten Boom wites of the aftermath of World War II.
> 'Since the end of the war I had had a home in Holland for victims of Nazi brutality. Those who were able to forgive their former enemies were able also to return to the outside world and rebuild their lives, no matter what the physical scars. Those who nursed their bitterness remained invalids. It was as simple and as horrible as that.'[4]

[1] S. Neill, p.211.
[2] F. Macnutt, *Healing* (Ave Maria Press, 1974) pp.171-2.
[3] K. Mitchell and H. Anderson, *All our losses, all our griefs* (Westminster Press, 1983) pp.129-130.
[4] C. ten Boom, *Tramp for the Lord* (Hodder and Stoughton and Christian Literature Crusade (1974) (1975 edition) p.57.

In *The Healing of Persons,* psychiatrist Paul Tournier gives a number of examples of the importance both of forgiving and of being forgiven in the process of healing of the former an interesting example is the case of 'Gilberte'. She had had a broken engagement, due to the infidelity of her fiancé. and the resentment she felt against him carried over into her relationship with her husband, whom she constantly accused of infidelity, which he stoutly denied. She was actually the victim of a 'paranoid obsession'. 'Gilberte's intuitive and sensitive nature, overexcited by her unresolved complexes, had made her too quick to see the tiniest gradation in her husband's affective behaviour. She had reached the point of being able to perceive infidelities hidden in his unconscious, of which he, being a simple, straightforward type, was unaware. And so she spoke of facts that were obvious to her, but which he denied simply because he could not see them. Argument only accentuated the two opposing attitudes . . .'. An experience of Christ on Easter Day cut the Gordian knot. 'When she came back to see me we prayed together. When she got to her feet she told me that she felt as if all her bitterness was falling away from her like a chain . . . She completely forgave, not only her husband, but also the fiancé who had been unfaithful to her in the past . . . Her face shone.'[1]

We have already noted the healing that came to 'Bridget'. For David Hamilton a former UVF man, the healing was just as effective. Challenged by a portion of Scripture left in his cell bed by a mate (to annoy him!) he prayed: 'God, if you are real, you come in and change me and take away this hatred.' Half-an-hour later he went straight up to the prison warder he was planning to kill and told him that he forgave him completely. When I met him five years later, David was a quietly-spoken, well-adjusted young man. The man who spoke of his former hatred as 'a cancerous growth in me' now says that 'there isn't an ounce of hatred left in my body.'

(b) Forgetting
'Forgetting wrong is an almost invariable accompaniment of forgiving, forgiving leads to forgetting and the forgiving process is not complete unless forgetting (not repressing) results.'[1]

If forgiving is hard, forgiving and forgetting is even harder. It sometimes requires a definite act of the will. There is a story told of Clara Barton, founder of the American Red Cross. 'A friend once reminded her of an especially cruel thing that someone had done to her years before. But Miss Barton seemed not to recall it. "Don't you remember it?" her friend asked. "No" came the reply, "I distinctly remember forgetting it." '[3]

Sometimes the subconscious is not so responsive. It may be necessary to repeat the original act of forgiveness when the memory of it is stirred. 'To forgive for the moment is not difficult,' says Lewis, 'but to go on forgiving, to forgive the same offence again every time it recurs to the memory—there's the real tussle.'[1]

[1] P. Tournier, *The Healing of Persons,* pp.253-255.
[2] D. Atkinson, 'The importance of forgiveness' in *Third Way* (Vol. 5 no. 10, October, 1982) p.7.
[3] A. L. McGinnes, *The Friendship Factor* (Quoted in *Family,* May, 1983 p.28).
[4] C. S. Lewis, *Letters to Malcolm: Chiefly on Prayer* (Geoffrey Bles, 1964; Fontana edition, 1966) pp.29-30.

Several writers refer to the danger of the line, 'I will forgive, but not forget'. The forgiver may feel that the offender remains in debt to him. Williams points out that 'We may in fact have forgiven—say, half-forgiven; and the pardon is thought to free the pardoner to every claim and compel the pardoned to every obedience.'[1] Michael Cassidy adds 'The trouble is that unless forgiveness is from the heart, it is like burying the hatchet but leaving the handle exposed so one can seize it again for further use at a later stage.'[2]

H. R. Mackintosh puts it like this:

'Those people who say that they can forgive but not forget betray the fact, unconsciously for the most part, that their "forgiveness" has been accompanied by reservations and qualifications which, morally, are fatal. It is of course true that the offending sin is remembered in the sense that we are still aware of it; ... But what has utterly changed for us is its value or personal significance. Before it was a fact that provoked and maintained estrangement; now, if pardon is real, the injured man has wholly ceased to regard that past event as determinative of his personal relationships to the offender. Self and neighbour are now at peace. In this sense all true forgiveness forgets the guilt which it pardons.'[3]

(c) Trusting

There is a story told of Thomas Edison, the inventor of the electric light bulb. After years of experiment Edison produced the first working bulb and handed it to his assistant, who promptly dropped it! After hours more work, Edison produced light bulb number two—and handed it straight to his assistant. Edison's trust showed that he had forgiven him.[4]

Trust and forgiveness do seem to go together. The forgiven Peter is given a job to do: 'Feed my sheep', Jesus tells him (John 21.17). An up-to-date experience of this kind is recounted by a correspondent. 'At this time', she writes, 'I found it very difficult to "be quiet" but for some reason I went upstairs to my bedroom . . . I just sat on my bed looking at a crucifix I had hung on the wall. . . . I think my mind was more or less blank when a voice beside me said, oh so clearly, "You are forgiven my child, I have work for you to do." '[5]

Sometimes, the renewal of trust takes time. Thus Kenneth Preston speaks about the restoration of the marriage relationship after an act of infidelity:

'A relationship which has been shattered by deeds can seldom be put right by words. Words will be needed, but without deeds they will not be believed. Usually it takes a deed to undo a deed. A trust that has been destroyed can only be restored gradually.

Supposing the husband is at fault. He must be encouraged to wait patiently until he has given his wife grounds for trusting him.

'It is sometimes difficult, even for the best of wives, to feel entire confidence in a husband once her confidence in him has been destroyed. But if he is prepared to be patient and to work hard to give her back her trust in him, then she in turn can make herself trust him.'[6]

---

[1] C. Williams, p.169.
[2] M. Cassidy, *Bursting the Wineskins* (Hodder and Stoughton, 1983), pp.14-15.
[3] H. R. Mackintosh, pp.33-34.
[4] From D. M. Prescott (ed.) *Further Stories for the Junior Assembly* (Blandford Press Ltd., 1974), The writer is indebted to the Rev. George R. Pike for this example.
[5] Private letter to the writer.
[6] K. Preston, *Marriage Counselling* (Library of Pastoral Care, SPCK, 1968) p.71.

And in a business or social situation, caution must be exercised. Suppose you have delegated a job to someone. He is to represent your firm at an important business meeting. You discover afterwards that he has let you down by ignoring your instructions, and the company has lost out as a result. Here is a problem: you may forgive him personally. You may trust him to act differently next time, on the basis that that action was out of character. But what about the other folk in the firm? Your forgiveness and trust might risk their wellbeing. So it is important to keep personal forgiveness and trust clearly distinguished from the social sphere in which there is responsibility to a wider group of people. Renewed trust is the aim of both forgiveness and pardon. However, in the social sphere it may be fairer to the individual, and to those affected by his failing, to 'test' his repentance by giving him repsonsibility in a different area from that in which he failed. This will enable him to re-establish himself in a less sensitive area, and give the wider grouping a chance to accept the reality of his repentance, and the subsequent rightness of trusting him in the area where he has failed.

(d) Reconciliation

We have already seen that forgiveness on the part of the victim may be very real without there being any sort of reconciliation. Sometimes reconciliation is not possible, because the wrongdoer has died or his whereabouts are unknown.

So Joseph Parker cannot be reconciled to those who killed his son, so long as they remain unknown to him. Nor, if he does find out their identity, can he be reconciled while they remain vindictive and unrepenting.

However, reconciliation is obviously one of the desired results of forgiveness. When reconciliation does take place, it must be realistic, as Smedes points out. So a divorced wife who forgives the husband who has run off with another woman cannot expect to relate to her former husband in the same way as when they were married. The reconciliation has to be in the context of her former husband's new relationship. Such realism demands real maturity.[1]

We have already seen, in the case of 'Bridget', that the reconciliation of brother and sister may entail an honest facing of personality differences which prevent their sharing each other's lives too closely.

In the case of Ken and the Australian doctor, we are not told the outcome of the mutual forgiveness at the 'miracle cross', but I imagine it led to a transformed working relaionship, and probably a deep friendship between two people who were formerly acquaintances at best. And what of Corrie ten Boom and the German guard? Surely an unforgettable bond was forged between two former enemies, though whether the relationship was actively maintained is open to question.

It is in the sphere of marriage that the need for straightforward reconciliation is most obvious. Festo Kivengere and his wife demonstrate the everyday forgiveness of small hurts which is needed to sustain a close relationship. Where deep-seated bitterness has crept in, there is the need for either a dramatic reversal, as in the case of 'Gilberte', or the more common gradual restoration of trust in which couples rebuild brick by brick the broken walls of their severed relationship.

[1] L. Smedes, pp.35-7.